SCRIPTURAL PRINCIPLES OF
GATHERING

SCRIPTURAL PRINCIPLES OF
GATHERING

ALFRED P. GIBBS

OR

WHY I MEET AMONG THOSE KNOWN AS BRETHREN

AN ADDRESS DELIVERED IN VANCOUVER, B.C, CANADA

WITH FOREWORD BY JOHN BLOORE

Originally Published by:
Walterick Publishers
P. O. Box 2216
Kansas City, Kansas 66110
Litho in U.S.A.

SCRIPTURAL PRINCIPLES OF GATHERING
By: ALFRED P. GIBBS
Copyright © 2012
GOSPEL FOLIO PRESS
All Rights Reserved

Published by
GOSPEL FOLIO PRESS
304 Killaly St. W.
Port Colborne, ON L3K 6A6
CANADA

Permission given by
ECS Ministries, April 4, 2011

www.gospelfolio.com

ISBN:9781926765679

Cover design by Danielle Elzinga

All Scripture quotations from the
King James Version unless otherwise noted.

Printed in USA

CONTENTS

Outline of Address 7

Foreword.. 11

Author's Preface to New Editions......................... 13

Introduction... 15

The Name of Gathering 19

Body of Christ which Christ is the Head 25

Word of God as Authority of Meeting................. 29

Person and Word of Christ.................................... 33

Welcome into the Assembly.................................. 35

Ordinances Observed.. 39

Priesthood of All Believers.................................... 45

Gospel Activity Based on God's Word 51

Conclusion.. 55

OUTLINE OF ADDRESS

Foreword by John Bloore
Preface by Alfred P. Gibbs

INTRODUCTION...15

1. The Purpose of the Address
2. The Necessity for the Address
3. The Question of One's Assembly or Church Association
4. Definition of the term: "Scriptural Principles of Gathering"
5. The World-wide Testimony of Assemblies of Believers
6. Should One remain in the Church Association in which He was Saved?

THE NAME OF GATHERING..19

FIRST: **They accepted no name but what is common to and inclusive of all believers and therefore refuse to recognize man-made and man-named sects and parties.**

1. There are no Sectarian Names in the New Testament
2. Scriptural Titles of Believers
3. Denominationalism Condemned in Scripture
4. Why Change the Title Christ has Given His Own?
5. Denominations Wrongly Likened to Various Regiments of an Army
6. Christian Unity not a Theory to be Sung About but a Reality to be Practiced
7. What Denomination does God's Word Advise one to Join?
8. What is a Sect?

BODY OF CHRIST WHICH CHRIST IS THE HEAD..25

SECOND: **They recognize and act upon the scriptural truth of the unity of the Church of God, which is the body of Christ, of which Christ is the Head and every believer a member.**

1. The Difference Between a Person Holding a Truth and that Truth holding a Person

2. The oneness of the body a scriptural revelation

3. The face of that one body and one Head excludes the necessity for other bodies with other heads

4. The Danger of wilful ignorance as to this unity

5. The local church, an expression of the church as a whole

WORD OF GOD AS AUTHORITY OF MEETING 29

THIRD: **They own no authority but the Word of God for their manner of meeting, and the maintenance of godly order in those meetings.**

1. We have no more right to invent a new way of gathering than we have to invent a new way of salvation

2. No description of a modern denomination in the New Testament

3. The local church according to the New Testament pattern

4. The scriptural gifts in the local assembly

5. Scriptural and unscriptural troubles

6. The right and wrong method of curing these troubles

7. Scriptural principles require scriptural power

PERSON AND WORK OF CHRIST..........................33

FOURTH: **They are uncompromisingly loyal to the Person and work of the Lord Jesus Christ.**

OUTLINE OF ADDRESS

1. Wrong doctrine tolerated in many denominations
2. What should be the attitude of a believer who finds himself in association with those who tolerate false doctrine?
3. Loyalty to the fundamentals of Christianity essential

WELCOME INTO THE ASSEMBLY 35

FIFTH: **They welcome into their assemblies all whom Christ has received, to the glory of God.**
1. Conditions in the early church
2. A mixed company in the assembly not contemplated in the New Testament
3. Discipline in the Local Assembly
4. The responsibility of those who see the truth

ORDINANCES OBSERVED 39

SIXTH: **They observe the ordinances, given to the Church by the Lord Jesus Christ, in a Scriptural manner.**
1. Baptism
   a. Its Symbolism
   b. Who should be baptized
   c. C. H. M.'s note on "Household Baptism"
   d. Is baptism a "non-essential"?
   e. Our attitude to those not scripturally baptized
2. The Lord's Supper
   a. The apostolic custom
   b. Its institution
   c. The weekly gathering for remembrance
   d. This scriptural ordinance should be observed in a scriptural manner

PRIESTHOOD OF ALL BELIEVERS............................45

SEVENTH: **They give liberty for the exercise of the priesthood of all believers, and have room for all the gifts of the risen Head to the Church.**

1. The false division of "clergy" and "laity"
2. The priesthood of all believers
3. The place and value of worship
4. The gifts to the Church
5. The bestowal, development, exercise, and recognition of the gifts
6. The evils of one-man ministry
7. The summary

GOSPEL ACTIVITY BASED ON GOD'S WORD...51

EIGHTH: **Their gospel activity is governed by the principles laid down in God's Word.**

1. Their foreign and home labourers
2. The liberty of the gospel preacher
3. The development of God-given ability possible in a scripturally ordered assembly

CONCLUSION..55

CONCLUDING REMARKS: **privilege carries with it responsibility.**

1. The advisability of acting upon what one knows to be the scriptural order of gathering
2. The responsibility of each believer to support the local assembly
3. The need for an open heart for all believers
4. The evils of a sectarian spirit
5. The believer should so study God's word that he may be able to help others to see and act upon this soul emancipating truth of the scriptural principles of gathering

FOREWORD

As the years pass and the Lord calls home those who have been used to bring out the essential teachings of God's Word as to the truth of the gospel and the scriptural order of the assembly, a new generation of believers grows up, many of whom are children of the Lord's people who come into the assemblies under circumstances quite different from their fathers. It is very needful that the fundamental principles relating to the fellowship of believers, as taught in Scripture, are freshly presented for their help and guidance.

This, too, may serve to enlighten others who may be exercised about the disorder, confusion and apostasy of Christendom, as these features are found in its existing religious organizations.

In the following pages this twofold service has been rendered in a worthy manner.

The reader will find that this booklet gives him, in simple language, a clear, concise and pointed statement of the teaching of Scripture as to the manner in which the Lord's people are to gather together; and in that connection the order it lays down as to reception, worship and ministry. In doing this, the author also makes plain the reasons for separation from the existing unscriptural sects and denominations of Christendom. Such as separation is indeed needful so that the will of God for His people may be carried out—a thing not possible in the religious systems of men with their humanly devised names, offices of service, ministry and ritual. Along with which in the main, gross indifference is found as to the faith and manner of life of those composing their organizations; and, as might be expected under such circumstances, they give shelter to the active propagators of evil doctrines by which the foundations of Christianity are attacked and efforts made to destroy the faith once delivered to the saints (Jude 3-4).

May all of us who know something of the spiritual liberty, godly care and soundness of doctrine found in the assemblies of God's people who gather together as described in this booklet, be stirred to a fuller appreciation of the association in which we are found; and, along with increasing gospel activity for the salvation of precious souls, seek to help and deliver our fellow believers that they may enjoy the same privileges.

—John Bloore

Plainfield, N.J., February, 1935.

AUTHOR'S PREFACE TO NEW EDITIONS

The kindly reception accorded to the previous editions of this pamphlet, which have had a wide circulation in this country and other English speaking lands, has been an encouragement to issue this revised edition with larger type. May the great Head of the Church be pleased to bless this simple setting forth of these *Scriptural Principles of Gathering*!

—A. P. G.

INTRODUCTION

This subject was chosen for the purpose of helping young believers of the various assemblies church truth. By "assembly truth" we mean, first, the scriptural warrant for the mode of gathering or assembling as believers; second, the Christian's position in that gathering; and third, the privileges and responsibilities of being so scripturally gathered.

God's Word thus enjoins the believer: *"Sanctify the Lord God in your hearts, and be ready always to give an answer to every man that asketh you a **reason** of the hope that is in you with meekness and fear"* (1 Pet. 2:15). Supposing the question that forms our topic were to be put to each believer associated with those known as "brethren," what would be the response? To the query: "Why do you meet with believers in this manner?" How many could give a scriptural reason for his position among believers called "brethren"? It is to be feared that many young believers, and old ones too, who could give a scriptural reason for their assurance of eternal salvation, could not give a similar reason for their assembly or church association. Surely one ought to be as necessary as the other. The One who has assured us of our salvation by His inspired Word has left us in no doubt, but that same Word, as to how and with Whom we should gather in church fellowship.

It has been felt by many that teaching along this line has been somewhat neglected of late; with that result we have a large number of young believers in our assemblies who do not know **why** they are **where** they are. They have little or no assured convictions as to the divine principles of gathering and, in many cases, are drifting hither and thither at the mercy of every impulse of men. Unlike the early disciples, they seem to have no definite link with a company which can be designated as *"their own company"* (Acts 4:23). In some quarters this line of ministry has been so over-emphasized to the exclusion of all else, that a spirit of sectarianism has been fostered which, of course, is equally to be deplored.

The first question that naturally arises after one is saved is: "Where shall I go, and with whom shall I meet for church fellowship?" There will be plenty of voices to advise. Some will reply: "Go where you can get spiritual food, no matter by what name they call themselves." Others will say: "Go to those with whom you will feel most at home with socially, where there are plenty of young folks and lots going on." Still others will respond: "Join the church of your preference, and be guided by your own tastes." The sincere believer, however, will not be guided be any such advice, but will rightly enquire: "Has the One who saved me by His grace and assured me of my blessedness by His Word given me no guidance, from the Bible, as to how and with whom I should meet?" He will then begin to search the Scriptures to discover what God has to say about this most important matter. It should be the solemn responsibility of each believer to so study the Word of God **for himself**. Only then can he be made absolutely certain that he is among those with whom the Lord would have him or her associate in assembly fellowship.

This introduces the subject of scriptural principles of gathering. As we shall use this expression quite frequently, let us define its meaning. But the word "principles" we mean that which is inherent in anything, determining its nature. It is a settled law or rule of action, especially of right action, consciously or resolutely adopted. It is the essential character of a thing, and the source from which a cause proceeds. We speak of "a man of principle," and by certain definite and right laws which motivate and control all his actions. A right principle is always right, whatever the circumstances surrounding the case may be. Neither time, place nor circumstances affect the correctness of a right principle.

By the word "scriptural" we mean that which has the **general** teaching of the Word of God, both by precept and practice, to support it. Note the phrase, "the **general** teaching of the Word of God." Most heresies can point to a verse of Scripture which **apparently** supports their contention, but when a heresy, or wrong doctrine, is examined in the light of **all** Scripture, its falsity is at once apparent. *"No... scripture is of any private interpretation"* (2 Pet. 1:20). This simply means that each statement of Scripture must be interpreted in the light of all the other scriptures bearing on that subject. This is a most important thing to remember when studying the Word of God.

By the word "gathering," we mean the coming together of believers for a distinct purpose, such as worship, prayer or the ministry of the word. We trust that the meaning of the phrase, "scriptural principles of gathering," has thus been made clear.

It may be good at this juncture to state that I was saved among those known as "brethren." This will probably be true of many readers. I never heard the clear unadulterated gospel of the grace of God until, at the age of twenty-one, I heard it through those known as "brethren." It may be of interest to state that, scattered throughout the world, there are many hundreds of companies of believers who meet simply as Christians to carry out those principles of gathering so clearly revealed in the Word of God. Wherever such a company gathers, a gospel testimony is maintained. By this means, thousands of precious souls have been led to a saving knowledge of the Son of God, Whom to know is eternal life. These companies, assemblies or gatherings of believers, because of their refusal to accept any name that is not common to and inclusive of all believers, have been called "brethren."[1] After I was saved I naturally desired to associate myself with those who had been instrumental, under God, in bringing me to a knowledge of the Lord Jesus Christ as my own personal Saviour.

This face, however, is not in itself a sufficient reason for linking oneself with, and remaining among a company of believers. As I began to study the Scriptures for myself, it became clear to me that those believers who had been used to lead me to Christ were also maintaining scriptural principles in their gatherings.

---

[1] The use of the term "brethren," throughout this book, must **never be understood** as a sectarian title that distinguishes certain believers from other Christians. This title is true of **all genuine believers** everywhere, by whatever other name they may call themselves.

The fact that one has been saved through the preaching of the gospel on the part of a certain group of people does not, in itself, justify a person remaining within the borders of that company, for there may be unscriptural things taught or practiced in that assembly that would prevent the young believer from growing in grace and in the knowledge of his Lord and Saviour, Jesus Christ.

Luther was saved while in the fold of the Roman Catholic Church. Should he therefore have remained in that certain ecclesiastical circle which both ignored and denied certain truths revealed in God's Word? Had all the Christians who were saved, while in the Romans Catholic church, remained therein, they would have been, humanly speaking, no Reformation, no Bible for the common people, no clear gospel and no liberty of scriptural thought and action such as we enjoy today. These men, for whom we should never cease to thank God, were not content to remain where God had saved them, but they searched the Scripture for themselves. When they discovered the unscripturalness of their assembly position, they separated themselves from that which did not conform to the truth of God's Word.

It would be well if every believer here were to give himself no rest until he has been assured by the infallible Book that the principles governing the assembly with whom he meets can stand the test of the general teaching of the Scriptures. Once this has been settled, he will never be happy or contented anywhere else. Young believers, get established, by a diligent study of the Word of God, in these scriptural principles of gathering! They will prove to be an anchor to your soul in these troublesome days of declension, denial, doubt and apostasy!

Now we come to the question before us, and it has been made a personal one: "Why do I meet with those known as 'brethren'?" We will try to answer it in as clear, simple and orderly a manner as possible, so as to leave no uncertainty in the minds of anyone present. We will state eight distinct reasons for being so gathered.

THE NAME OF GATHERING

FIRST: **They accept no name but what is common to and inclusive of all believers, and therefore refuse to recognize man-made and man-named sects and parties.**

We shall search our Bibles in vain to discover the "Baptist" denomination, or the "Presbyterian," the "Episcopalian," the "Congregational," the "Methodist" or a host of others we might name. Within each of these denominations there are very many genuine believers in our Lord Jesus Christ and, as such, we love them and gladly own them as members of the body of Christ; but we cannot love or own these denominations, for they are unscriptural in their formation, excluding many people of God. Is every believer in Christ a Baptist? An Episcopalian? A Lutheran? A Methodist? A Presbyterian? A Congregationalist? Of course not. These man-formed divisions **separate the people of God** into various distinct companies. With some it is an ordinance that distinguishes them, as with the "Baptists"; with others it is a form of church government, as "Presbyterian," or "Congregational." Others bear the name of the founder of that particular sect, such as "Lutherans" and "Wesleyans," but all such divisions are unscriptural.

When we open the pages of the New Testament we find that the people of God are called "Christians," "disciples," "saints," "believers," "brethren," etc. Are these titles true of all believers? Yes. Every child of God is a "Christian," a "saint," a "believer," a "disciple," and one of the "brethren." *"One is your Master, even Christ, and **all ye are brethren**,"* said the Lord Jesus (Matt. 23:8). But the term "brethren," therefore, **every true believer in**

Christ is included, and so with each of the other scriptural titles of God's people. The moment a person is saved, he is included among "the brethren," no matter what other man-made name he may be called, or call himself, later on.

Scripture unsparingly condemns denominationalism, or the dividing of the people of God into sects, parties and systems that exclude many Christians, who are sound in doctrine and life, from their fellowship. This spirit of sectarianism manifested itself early in the assembly at Corinth. Paul, by the Spirit of God, rebuked it and said: *"Ye are yet carnal, for whereas there is among you envying and strife and divisions* [or fractions]*, are ye not carnal and walk as men? For while one saith, 'I am of Paul'; and another 'I am of Apollos'; are ye not carnal? Who then is Paul, and who is Apollos, but ministers by whom ye believed?"* (1 Cor. 3:3-5). In the first chapter of that epistle he asks: *"Is Christ divided? Was Paul crucified for you, or were ye baptized in the name of Paul?"* (1 Cor. 1:13).

If Paul had been crucified for them, or had saved them, or they had been baptized in his name, then only had they the right to adopt his name as the founder of a party. Think of the hundreds of different denominations into which Christendom has been divided! Is this of God? We reply emphatically, "No, ten thousand times , no!" It is the work of **man** and the result, not of spirituality, but of **carnality**, which has scattered the people of God instead of uniting them! In that wonderful prayer, just before He went to the cross, our Saviour prayed that His people *"might be one; that the world may believe that Thou hast sent Me"* (John 17:21). The multiplicity of denominations certainly does not combine to present a spectacle of unity to the world, but rather of division and of confusion and worse confounded.

Many believers excuse their denominational affiliation by saying: "What's in a name? We're all out for the same thing. We'll all go to the same place!" These same believers would change their tune if someone forged their name to a check for a large amount and cashed it at their bank! What would be the reaction of these people if their wives suddenly decided to change their names and take another more suited to their poetic fancy? These husbands would rightly argue: "I gave you my name at our marriage, and you cannot change that name to suit yourself!" Why then should we alter the name that Christ has given to His own blood-bought people, and substitute it for another of our own making?

Many have sought to liken the various denominations of Christendom to the many different regiments of an army, each separate from the other, but all united for the common purpose of defending the country from invasion or attacking the enemy, as the head of the army orders. Such an illustration surely cannot apply in this case, for denominationalism is not content with the marching orders of the Commander-in-Chief, as found in His Word, but has substituted for them their own rules and regulations, and has thus virtually denied His supreme authority for faith and practice. The exhibition of rival denominations, each under a different flag, each commanded by a general of its own choosing, and each striving for the pre-eminence, it not calculated to suggest the unity of an army under the absolute control of a commander-in-chief!

Weekdays have often witnessed large congregations of believers singing heartily the beautiful words: "We are not divided, all one body we; one in hope and doctrine, one in charity." The dawn of Sunday, however, witnesses a sad contradiction to this blessed truth as each believer makes his way to his own particular denominational church building. To many, the words of that hymn were but the expression of a lovely **theory** to be **sung**, rather than a blessed **reality** to be **practiced** and enjoyed! The great truth, emphasized by the Spirit of God through Paul, needs to be proclaimed far and wide: *"Ye are all one in Christ Jesus"* (Gal. 3:28).

The story is told of two Christians who met for the first time in a railroad coach. After some pleasant conversation about the things of God, one inquired, "To what denomination do you belong?" The other replied, "That's just my difficulty, and I wish you would help me. Suppose you had only the Word of God to guide you, what denomination would you advise me to join?" His fellow Christian thought for a while and then said, "Why, if I had only the Word of God as my authority, I couldn't advise you to join any!" "That is exactly my position," responded the other, "and I therefore meet with those who act upon what they find written in the Word of God, and who seek to assemble in the name of the Lord Jesus Christ alone, apart from all the confusion that denominationalism has wrought." This is the position that those known as "brethren" occupy. They refuse to accept any name that is not inclusive of **every** believer, and firmly repudiate these man-made divisions and names that are not common to all the people of God.

It may be argued by some that these companies of so-called "brethren" are as much a sect as any other, but this is not true. The mere fact that a company of believers is called a sect does not make it so. Everything must be tested by the Word of God. Naturally, those in a sect will seek to justify themselves by calling others, who do not see eye to eye with them, a sect also.

Let us define the meaning of the word "sect." A sect is a body of people who make church claims, yet in principle and practice violate the essential principles of the Church of God as described in the New Testament Scriptures. In other words, a sect cannot stand the test of all Scripture. A sect usually adopts as its distinguishing features, some distinct form of ecclesiastical government, or some ordinance (or ordinances), or some particular doctrine, or the peculiar teaching of some person. Its conditions of membership cannot bear the light of the New Testament. It often allows unsaved people to enter its fold and excludes many Christians who do not see their way to subscribe to its particular creeds. It depends principally on its own rules and regulations, or "book of discipline," for its functioning and usually has a humanly ordained ministry and its own self-appointed oversight.

Those known as "brethren" unhesitatingly repudiate such pretensions, and seek to gather in accordance with the pattern described in the New Testament. Naturally they are thus distinguished from denominations, but they are not a sect, for they have no gathering centre but Christ; no name but what is common to and inclusive of all believers; no authority but the Word of God, and no conditions of reception to the local assembly but those found in the

Scriptures, namely: the person must be regenerated, be sound in the fundamental doctrines of Scripture, and be living a clean moral life before the world that commends the gospel.

It has been well pointed out that in the early days of Christianity there were congregations of believers, but no "Congregationalists"! There were baptized believers, but no "Baptists"! There were presbyters, or elders, in the assembly, but no "Presbyterians"! They had method in their meetings, but there were no "Methodists"! They had bishops in the church, but there were no "Episcopalians"! They trembled at the Word, but there were no "Quakers"! They all shared in the blessings of Pentecost, but there were no "Pentecostalists"! The brethren had all been united to Christ, but there were no "United Brethren"! They met simply as Christians, in the name of the Lord Jesus Christ, and were obedient to His precious Word.

BODY OF CHRIST WHICH CHRIST IS THE HEAD

SECOND: **They recognize and act upon the scriptural truth of the unity of the Church of God, which is the Body of Christ, of which Christ is the Head, and every believer a member.**

Notice those words "**recognize** and **act upon**." Every intelligent believer, whatever his denominational affiliation may be, would be willing to **recognize** and concede that Scripture reveals the existence of but one Church, with Christ as its Head and every believer as a member. But comparatively few seem prepared to follow this revelation to its logical conclusion, and **act** upon this truth, cost what it may and lead where it will. It is one thing for a person to hold a truth, and another for that truth to so hold him that it causes him to regulate his conduct by it.

The Scriptures make plain that there is but one Church, which is called *"the body of Christ,"* of which He is the Head and every believer is a member. The Word of God is very definite as to this. Listen to these quotations from the Bible: *"So we* [believers], *being many, are **one body** in Christ, and every one **members one of another"** (Rom. 12:5). *"For as the body is **one**, and hath many members, and all the members of that **one** body, being many, are **one** body, so is Christ"* (1 Cor. 12:12). *"There is **one** body and one Spirit"* (Eph. 4:4). *"Now ye* [believers] *are the body of Christ and members in particular"* (1 Cor. 12:27).

Each regenerated person is described, in Scripture, as having been joined, by the Spirit of God, to the body of Christ, the Church. *"By one Spirit are we all baptized into **one body"*** (1 Cor. 12:13). Each believer is not only united by the Holy Spirit to the **Head** in heaven, but is also united to **every other** believer on earth in whom the Spirit of God dwells. This is the great truth of the unity of the body. Christ is thus linked eternally with His own, and they, in turn, are described as being *"all one in Christ Jesus"* (Gal. 3:28).

Since there is but **one** body of which Christ is the Head, then there is obviously no room in the world for **many** bodies with many heads, as exemplified by denominationalism today. Seeing there is but **one** body of which every believer is a member, with Christ as the Head, what necessity is there for forming other bodies with men at their head? No one can "join" the church, which is the body of Christ, any more than one's finger can "join" his body. As the finger has joined to the body at physical birth, so the believer is said to be **joined** to the body by the Spirit of God at spiritual birth (1 Cor. 6:17; Eph. 4:16; Col. 2:19). Thus it is clearly seen that the Church is not an organization **to be joined**, but an organism (the body of Christ) to which every believer **has been joined**. Let us underline this fact in our minds.

Since, therefore, there is but **one** Church, to which every believer has been joined, why try to join oneself to another? Is not what God has joined together good enough? Is not the Headship of Christ sufficient for the Church? Is not the Word of God of sufficient authority? Those who are called "brethren" recognize and act upon the scriptural truth of the one body, and seek, not to **form another body, but to own as sufficient what God has already formed**. They therefore meet together as members of the body of Christ, in subjection to the authority of the Head, and in accordance with the principles He has laid down in His own Word. Could anything be simpler, or more scriptural than this? We are nowhere told to **make** a unity but, on the contrary, we are entreated to *"keep the unity of the Spirit* [which God has already made] *in the bond of peace"* (Eph. 4:3). How anyone, who has really grasped the truth of the one body and the one Head, can continue in a denominational affiliation, is a problem that only the judgement seat of Christ can solve.

It is one thing to be ignorant of the true character of sectarianism, which virtually denies the truth of the one body; and

26

it is another to **remain** in such association after one has been enlightened as to its unscriptural character. When a Christian is unaware of the fact that a denomination is contrary to God's Word, his conscience is undefiled and God can use him; but the fact that God uses such a one must not be interpreted as proof that God approves of his denominational position. As long as a man walks according to the light he has, he will be blessed; but woe betide the man who sees the evils and unscripturalness of denominationalism, and yet **remains** in it! "Light accepted bringeth light; but light rejected bringeth night," — and how great is the darkness of willful ignorance!

Each local church, or assembly of believers, represents and expresses (or should represent and express) the church as a **whole**, even as a tiny dewdrop reflects in miniature the same sky as the mighty ocean. Each local assembly therefore should have Christ as its Head, believers only as its members, the Word of God as its guide, the Holy Spirit for its Power, and the glory of Christ as its objective.

Does the company with whom you meet thus recognize and act upon the truth of the oneness of all believers in Christ; or does it create artificial barriers that shut out regenerated believers who are sound in doctrine and moral in their lives? Such a company **is not contemplated in the New Testament**, and therefore has no scriptural authority for its constitution, existence and perpetuation. The "brethren" seek to hold and practice this truth so clearly revealed in the Book of books, and therefore have scriptural authority for their position.

WORD OF GOD AS AUTHORITY OF MEETING

THIRD: **They own no authority but the Word of God for their manner of meeting, and the maintenance of godly order in those meetings.**

Like the Bereans of old they have *"received the word with all readiness of mind, and **searched** the Scriptures daily whether those things were so"* (Acts 17:11). They believe that they have no more right to make a new mode of meeting for the Lord's people than they have to make a new way of salvation. Since the way of salvation, give by divine inspiration nearly two thousand years ago, is good and sufficient for today, then God's principles of gathering, revealed in the same book, are just as necessary for our guidance in assembly fellowship as they were in the days of old. We cannot improve on the pattern God has given His people in the New Testament. Do you believer this? The "brethren" do and **act** on it.

We would search the New Testament in vain to discover anything described therein that approximates a denomination of today, which selects one man as its minister to do all its preaching, teaching, praying and the leading of its worship; which calls itself by some man-given title; which is regulated by its own by-laws and books of discipline; which has its own creed, to which all must subscribe so they can join; which in many cases, has added rites and ordinances and ceremonies the Word of God knows nothing about, and which often allows unsaved people to join and remain in its fellowship. This is not a distortion of facts, as a visit to and an examination of many denominational organizations will soon convince the sincere inquirer.

A reading of the New Testament, especially Acts, will reveal the fact that believers, and **believers only**, gathered together in the name of the Lord Jesus Christ (Matt. 18:20); for remembrance of the Lord in the breaking of bread (Acts 20:7; 1 Cor. 11:23-24); for edification (Acts 2:14-47; 1 Cor. 12-14 chapters); and for prayer, etc. (Matt. 18:20; Acts 4:23-30). These companies, whether large or small, are called "churches" or "assemblies." We find the expression, *"Churches of the saints"* (1 Cor. 14:33), *"Churches of God"* (1 Thess. 2:14), *"Churches"* (Acts 9:31; 15:41; 16:5), and *"Churches of Christ"* (Rom. 16:16).

In these churches, or assemblies of believers, there is **no mention** of "the minister," or "the book of discipline," or "the creed," or any special name such as "Baptist," "Presbyterian," etc. by which these assemblies were distinguished from each other. It was merely their **location** that distinguished them. We find *"The church of God which is at **Corinth**"* (1 Cor. 1:2), "The churches of **Galatia**" (Gal. 1:2), etc. The church which was at Corinth included all the believers in Christ in that city. A letter addressed "To the church of God in Chicago," or any other city you wish to name, **would apply to and include every regenerated person in that city**, for that term includes all who have been joined to the body of Christ by the Spirit of God.

In the Church, which is His body, Christ the Head has given certain gifts for the edification, or building up, of the whole body of believers. These gifts are evangelists, pastors and teachers (Eph. 4:8-16). These are recognized in and discharge their ministry in and with the fellowship of the local assemblies. Then also there are bishops (or elders) and deacons, in these churches, as for example in Philippi (Phil. 1:1). There is no mention whatever of **one man** in charge, to whom the assembly delegated the task of teaching, preaching and shepherding. There is no such term as "the pastor of a church" or "the teacher, or preacher of a church." The word is always in the **plural**, except where the requirements and responsibility of the work is described. In the same assembly there were pastors, evangelists, teachers, bishops and deacons. How does this fit in with what is seen in modern denominationalism?

If a person were to examine the New Testament to discover how to get rid of "the pastor of a church," he would discover that there was no such person described, or even contemplated therein. There are two kinds of troubles from which a company of believers may suffer: scriptural and unscriptural. The former can be dealt with according to the directions of the Bible; but the latter must be decided by the by-laws and discipline books of men. Scripturally gathered companies of God's people have their troubles (for the flesh is within them as it is among all the other "brethren in Christ"), but these troubles are anticipated and the remedy provided by the Word of God.

For example, a company of believers have failed in acting toward one another in love. Jealousy and strife have been allowed to remain unjudged in the assembly; the Holy Spirit is grieved and crushed, and confusion and barrenness follows. What is the remedy? There are two methods. One is for every believer in that assembly to humble himself before God in confession of his sin and restitution to his brethren, and God will be pleased to come in and revive the assembly of believers with the conscious sense of His presence and the liberty and power of the Holy Spirit. The other method is to appoint one man as the head of that assembly, and allow him to have the management of the meeting, the responsibility for the ministry of the Word, the dispensing of the Lord's Supper, the conducting of the prayer meeting and the preaching of the gospel so that all confusion will be brought to an end.

Which is the right method of restoration, the first or the last? Such a question has only one reply. Every child of God will agree that the first method is honouring to God and is the scriptural remedy. The other method is seen in denominationalism with its attendant evils of clerisy, hierarchies, synods, councils, books of discipline, etc.

It cannot be emphasized sufficiently that **scriptural principles of gathering require scriptural power**—the Holy Spirit—for their operation. When that power is absent, confusion follows; but it is not the principles that have failed, but the **people**. Once the people of God are restored in heart, the power will once more be apparent. The principles, being scriptural, are always true and right. Let us not adjust the **principles** of God's Word to our form of **gathering**, but our form of **gathering** to the **principles** found in the good Book. Is this clear? So long as the flesh remains in the people of God, there will be manifestations of it which will make painful history; but the **principles of Scripture remain unchanged** and **unchangeable**. The apostle Paul, in 1 Corinthians 14, rebuked the Corinthians believers for their shameful behaviour in the assembly, which had resulted in disorder and disgrace; but never for one moment did he suggest that those scriptural **principles**, which he had delivered to them, be revised to suit their carnal ideas and backslidden condition of soul.

PERSON AND WORD OF CHRIST

FOURTH: **They are uncompromisingly loyal to the Person and work of the Lord Jesus Christ.**

In other words, they seek to hold, or acknowledge the supreme authority and headship of Christ (Col. 1:18; 2:19). Nothing derogatory to the Person and work of Christ would be allowed to remain unchallenged and unjudged for one moment in their assemblies, and this is true the world over, wherever these scripturally constituted gatherings are found. The essential deity of the Son of God (as coequal and coeternal with the Father and the Holy Spirit) and the necessity for the efficacy of the substitutionary sacrifice of Christ as the only ground for the believer's acceptance before God is emphasized constantly in their assemblies.

Those who meet among those known as "brethren" may not be noted for their oratorical gifts, but one thing is certain: wherever one stands up to preach the gospel, Christ's Person is exalted, His eternal deity is confessed and the all-sufficiency of the work of redemption, which He accomplished by the shedding of His precious blood, is proclaimed with no uncertain sound.

It would be good if this were true of all denominational gatherings, but alas, it is more often the exception than the rule! Men are allowed on the pulpits of many church buildings who deny the deity of Christ, scoff at the doctrine of redemption through His blood, and belittle or refuse to accept the Bible as the divinely inspired and therefore absolutely inerrant and authoritative Word of God. The tragedy is that many professing Christians appear to see no inconsistency in listening to this denial of their Lord and this travesty of the gospel. By their very membership, presence and financial support of such an organization, they thus help to perpetuate this disgraceful thing! The deity of Christ is the **foundation stone of Christianity**. The person who denies Christ's deity **is not a Christian**, and therefore has no place whatever in a professedly Christian pulpit. Any company of people that tolerates a preacher who denies Christ's deity and His redemptive work is no place for a true and faithful child of God. If Christ is not God, we do not **need** Him. Since Christ is God, we **cannot** do without Him!

To continue in a company of professed believers that permits doctrinal evil to be preached and remain unjudged is disloyalty to the Person and work of the Lord Jesus Christ. To continue in such an association is to give one's support to it. The Word of God is clear as to the attitude of a believer in such a case. *"What part that he that believeth with an unbeliever? ... Wherefore* **come out from among them**, *and be ye separate, saith the Lord and touch not the unclean thing; and I will receive you, and will be a Father unto you, and ye shall be My sons and daughters saith the Lord almighty"* (2 Cor. 6:15-18). *"Evil communications corrupt good manners,"* declares the Bible (1 Cor. 15:33). A man is known by the company he keeps. It is far better for a person to stand alone for what he knows to be the truth of the Holy Scripture and the honour of God's Son, than to be linked by membership with the enemies and blasphemers of his blessed Lord.

Loyalty to the commander-in-chief is essential to the united attack of an army against a common enemy. What would you think of those in an army who were afraid to face the foe lest some of their own number should plunge a bayonet into their backs? This is the situation in many denominations, where loose and blasphemous views of the Person and work of the Son of God are tolerated. A member of such an organization never knows when the deity of his Lord will be attacked from behind the pulpit, the efficacy of His precious blood ridiculed and denied, and the truth and authority of God's Word questioned. Thank God, such is not true among the thousands of assemblies of believers known as "brethren" scattered throughout the whole world.

WELCOME INTO THE ASSEMBLY

FIFTH: **They welcome into their assemblies all whom Christ has received, to the glory of God.**

All regenerated persons who are sound in doctrine and godly in their walk before the world are welcomed. To make any other conditions for welcoming a person to the Lord's Supper and the privileges of the assembly is **to act in a sectarian manner** that has no scriptural warrant, and which only serves to bring confusion and dishonour to a company of believers.

A reading of the book of Acts and the Epistles will indicate that the early churches were composed of professed believers only and were not a mixture of saved and unsaved. With these assemblies each believer associated himself upon his conversion. There was no need for a person to ask in that day: "What denomination shall I join?" There was only one place for the child of God to go, and that was where believers met together in the name of the Lord Jesus, either for prayer, praise, worship, or the ministry of the Word.

On the day of Pentecost, those who gladly received the Word were baptized and added to the assembly that had already been formed by the Spirit of God (Acts 2:41). Peter and John, after their arrest and acquittal, *"went to their own company"* (Acts 4:23). We are told: *"And of the rest* [the unsaved] *durst no man join himself to them"* (Acts 5:13). Simon, a false professor, was told by Peter that he had *"no part nor lot in this matter"* (Acts 8:18-23). Saul of Tarsus, after his conversion, *"was with the disciples certain days"* (Acts 9:19). When he *"assayed to join himself to the disciples"* at Jerusalem, the believers were afraid to receive him because he had been such an enemy of Christians. Barnabas, however, vouched for the reality of his Christian profession and character, and he was then gladly welcomed (Acts 9:26). This is the story all through the Acts. The apostle Paul was greatly used of God, through the preaching of the gospel and teaching of the Word, in establishing little assemblies of believers who met together in the name of the Lord Jesus Christ. To these local assemblies every Christian, who was doctrinally and morally sound, was gladly welcomed.

In the early days of Christianity, it was the custom for a believer, who left one town to go to another, to take with him a letter from his home assembly, commending him to the love and care of the assembly in the town to which he was going (2 Cor. 3:1). By this means it was made reasonably certain that believers only met at the Lord's Supper to show forth the Lord's death. While a letter of commendation serves a good and useful purpose, it must not be allowed to become a rigid rule or made an essential condition for a believer to be welcomed to the Lord's Supper. This is mere formalism. It is with **principles** and not **rules** that the New Testament concerns itself in this matter. The spectacle of saved and unsaved, linked together by a common membership of church fellowship, such as we see around us in Christendom, has no counterpart in the New Testament. We read there that *"all that believed were together"* (Acts 2:44).

The "brethren" have sought to return to these New Testament principles of gathering, and no unsaved person is knowingly permitted to partake of the Lord's Supper or allowed to associate with them in their assembly fellowship. Neither is any person who is unsound in the fundamentals of God's Word or who is morally wrong in his life permitted to continue with them in church fellowship. If any person in their assemblies is proven, **after careful and unbiased examination**, to hold and teach wrong doctrine, or is immoral in his life, or guilty of the sins enumerated in 1 Corinthians 5:11, he is put away from that assembly until such time as it is quite clear he has been restored in heart to the Lord (1 Cor. 5:11-13; 2 Cor. 2:6-8).

WELCOME INTO THE ASSEMBLY

The "brethren" rightly argue that as the Lord's Supper belongs to the Lord, it is for the Lord's people only. The Lord only invites His own blood-bought people to thus remember Him. An assembly of believers simply **welcomes** the Christian who is sound in life and doctrine, and who has seen from the Word of God his privilege and responsibility to be there. If, from what you have seen and heard from God's Word, you have been brought to realize that your place is among those who meet thus in the name of the Lord Jesus Christ alone, in scriptural simplicity, and apart from the ecclesiastical forms invented by men, make known this desire to an assembly of believers. They, in turn, will interview you to see whether you can give a reason for the hope that is within you, and whether you are sound in life and doctrine. Once this is established, they will gladly welcome you to share with them the Christian fellowship and assembly privileges that are the birthright of every true believer in Christ.

ORDINANCES OBSERVED

SIXTH: **They observe the ordinances, given to the Church by the Lord Jesus Christ, in a scriptural manner.**

These ordinances are two in number: baptism and the Lord's Supper; the first is administered to the believer **once**, the second observed by the believer **often**.

BAPTISM is the God-ordained **figure**, symbol or picture of the believer's death, burial and resurrection with Christ. By his baptism with water the Christian confesses his identification with the Lord Jesus Christ in His death, and his determination to walk in newness of life to the glory of Him who went under the waves and billows of God's wrath to deliver him from the penalty and power of sin, and from the present evil world (Psalm 22:1-21; 88:1-18; Rom. 6:1-14; Gal. 1:4).

The Saviour's commission to His disciples was: *"Go ye therefore and make disciples of all nations, baptizing them in the name of the Father, and of the Son, and of the Holy Spirit; teaching them to observe all things whatsoever I have commanded you, and lo, I am with you always, even unto the end of the world* [age]*"* (Matt. 28:19-20). In obedience to this commission, those known as "brethren" have gone forth with the gospel. When souls have been won for Christ, the truth of baptism has been placed before them, and the believers have been baptized, or immersed in water, symbolizing their burial with Christ.

There is no such thing taught in the New Testament as baptism before profession of faith on the part of the individual. The scriptural order of Christian baptism is: *"He that* **believeth** *and is* **baptized***"* (Mark 16:16). Search the history of the Church as found in the Acts of the Apostles, and you will not find **one case of infant baptism** recorded. Baptism is conditioned upon believing, which comes through an intelligence of the gospel (Rom. 10:6-17). Surely this cannot be true of a helpless babe in arms!

Of the theory of so-called "Household Baptism" (which teaches that each member of the household of a believer, **including the infants of the home**, should be baptized), we cannot do better than quote C. H. Macintosh, author of the world famed and greatly used *Notes on the Pentateuch*, who wrote on December 22, 1871:

> "I believe the course of some of our friends in urging this question of [household] baptism will, unless God in His mercy interpose, lead to most disastrous results. For my own part, seeing the question has been thus forced upon me, I can only say I have, forty-two years, been asking in vain for a single line of Scripture for baptizing any save believers, or those who profess to believe. I have had inferences, conclusions and deductions; but of direct Scripture authority, not a tittle."

Many Christians seem to regard water baptism as a **"non-essential,"** and treat it with indifference by saying: "Well, it doesn't affect one's salvation, so why worry?" But surely the distinct command of the Lord Jesus is not a non-essential for a believer. It is true that baptism does not secure the soul's eternal salvation and acceptance before God, but surely it is necessary to be in complete obedience to the Lord Jesus Christ if He declared it should be done. Though the Lord puts the responsibility to carry out His command to baptize directly upon those who preach the gospel (Matt. 28:18; Mark 16:15-16), it is fitting that the believer should be prayerfully exercised about having this divinely-appointed ordinance carried out in the way that Scripture teaches, especially in view of the deep spiritual significance attached to it by the apostle Paul. Read Romans 6:1-14 carefully.

While maintaining firmly that baptism by immersion, sub-sequent to a profession of faith in Christ, is the plain teaching of the New Testament, we should be careful not to make this ordinance **the door of admittance** to and participation in the Lord's Supper. Nor should we make it the basis for offering the privilege of gathering in scriptural simplicity of our fellowship with other Christians, who have not yet been brought to see from God's Word the distinctive truths of believer's baptism.

We must ever keep in mind the fact that we are living today in the midst of something the New Testament does not contemplate: a baptized mass of humanity. Practically every genuine Christian we meet has passed through some form of so-called baptism. In a great number of cases, he was sprinkled with water as an infant. When, in later years, he was saved by the grace of God, he imagined that this christening was the equivalent of believer's baptism, and his denomination encourages him in this belief.

By all means, let us place before such, in a kindly, courteous and Christian way, the teaching of God's Word as to these things; but, at the same time, let us never forget that every believer is a child of God and a fellow member of the body of Christ. May it be ours to extend to all those who *"belong to Christ"* (Mark 9:41) that Christian love, care and forbearance that the Head of the body declared were the marks of true discipleship (John 13:34-35; cp. 1 John 3:14, 16; 4:20; 5:1).

Many a godly Christian has stumbled because of the harsh, hyper-critical, uncharitable and contemptuous attitude shown towards him by a better taught believer, or company of believers, who failed utterly to take into consideration his spiritual environment. Let us ponder carefully and prayerfully the words of the inspired apostle: *"Owe no man anything, but to **love** one another"* (Rom. 13:8), and, *"Wherefore **receive ye** one another, as Christ also received us, to the glory of God"* (Rom. 15:7).

THE LORD'S SUPPER, as we have already seen, is for all the Lord's people who are sound in life and doctrine. An examination of the practice of the early Church, as seen in the book of Acts, seems to indicate that brethren of a given community came together **each Lord's day** to show forth the Lord's death in the breaking of bread (Acts 20:7). They came primarily, not to hear preaching, but to break the bread, symbolic of the body of their Lord and Saviour; and drink the cup, symbolic of His precious blood.

For this ordinance also we have abundant Scripture testimony. The very night in which Christ was betrayed, He gathered His disciples together and instituted this feast of remembrance (see Luke 22:19-20; Matt. 26:26-28; Mark 14:22-25). From John 13, it seems certain that Judas left after the Passover feast, and before the Lord's supper was instituted. In 1 Corinthians 11:23-34, this ordinance of the Lord's Supper is given by the glorified Lord, as a distinct revelation to Paul the apostle. It is introduced because the brethren in Corinth had abused the privilege of the Lord's Supper by turning it into a feast in which every man satisfied his own appetite for food and drink. The purpose and propriety of this blessed ordinance is there stated as a direct revelation from the ascended Lord in glory, and every Christian should read and re-read this whole passage carefully and prayerfully.

Some think that in the primitive Church this feast was celebrated each day (Acts 2:46); but by the time assemblies were spread throughout Asia, it became the established custom for the disciples to come together the first day of the week to break bread (Acts 20:7). Notice the expression used. It was not the first Sunday of the month, or the first Sunday of the quarter, or the first Sunday of the half-year, or the year, but the **first day of the week**. The same term is used again in 1 Corinthians 16:1-2, where Paul, speaking of the collection for the saints says: *"Upon the first day of the week, let each of you lay by him in store as the Lord has prospered him."* The primary purpose of these believers, in assembling themselves together on the first day of the week in the name of the Lord Jesus Christ was to remember Him in His own Divinely appointed way, and thus *"proclaim the Lord's death until He come."*

This is what those called "brethren" still seek to do. Throughout the world at a time most convenient to the majority of the believers, Christians, and **Christians only**, gather together in the Lord's name alone. In their midst is a table upon which is placed a loaf of bread and a cup containing the fruit of the vine. Inasmuch as it is the **Lord's supper**, there is no one present who attempts to usurp the lordship and authority of Christ by attempting to take His place or to arrange its program. One after another of the brethren arise as the Spirit leads—one with a hymn, another voicing the worship of the assembly, another with some Scripture exposition in keeping with the feast of remembrance. One rises to give thanks for the bread, and it is broken and passed so that all may break it and eat. Perhaps another rises to give thanks for the cup and in turn it is passed from one to the other.

Thus, in scriptural simplicity, this feast, instituted by the Saviour, is kept. There is no **visible** head at this feast of remembrance for none such is contemplated in Scripture. However Christ is there according to His promise: *"Where two or three are gathered together in My name, there am I in the midst of them,"* and who would dare to take His place? This is what clerisy has done and, whether consciously or unconsciously, Christ's place of pre-eminence in the assembly of His saints for worship has been superseded by the so-called "minister," who has been humanly ordained, who "dispenses the elements" and, **apart from whose presence**, the Lord's Supper cannot be partaken and enjoyed! From such a travesty of the pattern given in the New Testament we turn with abhorrence. Scripture makes clear that Christ is the Host at His own table, and each believer is His greatly privileged and highly honoured guest.

There is no greener spot on the face of the wilderness of a world in which the believer's lot is cast, than when believers meet around the Lord, each Lord's day, to remember the Lord Jesus Christ in the Lord's own appointed way, proclaiming the Lord's death until the Lord comes back again. Is this your happy privilege, fellow believer? Rest not until it is, and you can truthfully sing:

"Lord Jesus, in Thy precious name,
And, in that name alone;
At Thy request we gladly meet,
Thy Lordship here would own.

As on that dark betrayal night,
Thou didst this feast ordain;
We too, the bread and cup would take,
Thy death, Lord, thus proclaim.

The bread, Thy body doth portray;
The cup, Thy precious blood;
By which our sin was put away,
Our peace was made with God.

The Host art Thou, O blessed Lord,
Thy honoured guests are we;
With grateful and adoring hearts,
We would remember Thee!

Lord Jesus, Whom, unseen we love,
As thus we muse on Thee;
We none would see, save Thee alone,
Thou Man of Calvary!"

PRIESTHOOD OF ALL BELIEVERS

SEVENTH: **They give liberty for the exercise of the priesthood of all believers, and have room for the development of all the gifts given by the risen Head to His Church.**

The abominable heresy that divides the church of God into two classes, called the "clergy" and the "laity," is utterly unknown in the New Testament. This did not come into existence until the latter part of the second century, as a perusal of any reliable "church history" will prove. This innovation was undoubtedly the work of the Devil, and it has wrought untold havoc in the church of God. The word "clergy" comes from the word *kleeros*, which is translated, "heritage." In 1 Peter 5:3 the Spirit of God declares that all believers are God's *kleeros*, or heritage. The term "laity" comes from the word *laos*, which means "the common people."

In Christendom today we hear of "clergymen and laymen," or the *kleeros* and the *laos*. The clergymen belongs to a particular class in the Church and, by reason of education along certain religious lines plus human ordination, has authority conferred upon him to preach, baptize, administer the elements in the Lord's Supper, and also lead the congregation in public worship, prayer and ministry, as well as shepherd the flock. The layman, not being so educated and ordained, has no such privileges, and must be content to occupy a subordinate place. This detestable heresy finds it fullest expression in the Roman Catholic Church, but Protestantism also is greatly corrupt by it.

There is not the slightest ground for this division of Christians in the New Testament. You will search in vain for it. It is foreign to the whole language of Scripture in which **every believer** is viewed as a *"priest"* (1 Pet. 2:5-9). As such he is exhorted to *"offer up spiritual sacrifices, acceptable to God by Jesus Christ"* (1 Pet. 2:5). **All** God's people are described as being constituted a kingdom of priests unto God (Rev. 1:5, 6; 5:10). **All** are invited to draw near with a true heart, in full assurance of faith through *"the great high Priest of their confession,"* whose blood has opened up the new and living way into God's presence and favour (Heb. 10:19-22).

The elaborate ritual of Judaism, with its special priesthood, **was done away in Christ!** The veil has been rent, and every regenerate person has been constituted a priest unto God. All enlightened Christians will acknowledge this, yet many continue to maintain their membership in a system which both recognizes and supports this multitude of unscriptural "reverends," "right reverends," etc., etc. Inasmuch as the church of God is likened to a human body, each part of being necessary for the proper functioning of the whole; there can therefore be no division of the body into two separate bodies or classes, such as is practiced in most circles of denominationalism.

Among those known as "brethren," no such distinctions are tolerated for one moment. As they meet as an assembly for worship or prayer, all the believers occupy the same common ground of priesthood, and liberty is given to the Spirit of God to express Himself **audibly** through any of the **men** so gathered, the **women** being expressly enjoined to be *"silent in the churches"* (1 Cor. 14:34-35).

In such gatherings, worship is given its proper place. Christendom has practically eliminated the place of the worship meeting, where believers gather for the purpose of giving God that which He is seeking from His people, the worship of their hearts. Worship is not prayer for one's needs or praise for one's blessings, but the overflow of the soul in adoration to God for what He is in Himself, as revealed by the Lord Jesus Christ. Prayer is the occupation of the heart with its needs; praise, the occupation of the heart with its blessings; but worship is the occupation of the heart with God Himself.[2] How little of this is found in Christendom and denominationalism, and God is consequently robbed of His portion from His people!

While it is quite true that all believers are priests—it is also true that not all are evangelists, pastors, or teachers. These are gifts, given to the church by the ascended Head. But the fact that one of the believers exercises either of these gifts does not place him in a superior class above his brethren: he merely exercises the gift he has been given as part of the body of Christ, and thus the whole assembly is edified and build up. In the assembly, as a whole, there are evangelists, pastors and teachers. As such they are not limited to any one church. There is no such thing as **the** evangelist of a church, or **the** pastor of a church, or **the** teacher of a church. Bishops and deacons are local in their sphere. As regards the bishop, he is a very different person from what we know of that high ecclesiastical office as found in the sects of Christendom. The acceptance of this truth would greatly upset some of the highly organized denominations of today.

The "brethren" seek to **recognize** and give liberty for the exercise of these gifts in the assembly. They believe that God meant what He said when He declared: *"As every man hath received the gift, even so minister the same one to another, as good stewards of the manifold grace of God"* (1 Pet. 4:10-11). A gift will make room for itself, and it will soon become apparently to the assembly whether a person really has the gift of an evangelist, a teacher or a pastor. The saints are exhorted to *"know, or recognize, them that labour among them"* (1 Thess. 5:13), but are never asked to **elect, choose,** or **appoint** them. With the **business** affairs of an assembly, however, this is different (Acts 6:1-4).

Christendom presents the spectacle of one man being elected and appointed by a congregation for a certain stipulated salary to do all the evangelism, teaching and shepherding of the flock; but seldom indeed is there a person who has all these gifts combined in himself. Furthermore, Scripture does not contemplate

---

2   See author's book on *Worship, the Christian's Highest Occupation.* Walterick Publishers. Kansas City, Kansas.

a stipulated salaried ministry. The New Testament knows nothing of a minister hired to preach at so much per annum. It is foreign to New Testament principles, which describes the evangelist, teacher, or pastor, who is devoting his whole time to such a ministry, as looking alone to the Lord for his support (1 Cor. 9:14). We need not to be surprised by attacks on the part of so-called "ministers" of denominations against the "brethren." These men realize that if they accepted what the "brethren" practice along this line, both their position and salary would be lost. Their opposition is simply a gesture of self-defense to defend a system from which they derive a livelihood (3 John 7).

The idea of taking collections of money from a mixed audience of saved and unsaved has also no scriptural warrant. *"Freely ye have received, freely give,"* was our Saviour's exhortation (Matt. 10:8). There is not the slightest suggestion in the New Testament of money being solicited from unsaved people to "help the cause," or to "pay the minister's salary," or to "pay off the mortgage on the house of God." The collections of money were to be taken from the **Lord's people only** (1 Cor. 16:1-2). What shame and disgrace Christendom has brought to the name of Christianity, by using worldly means to extract money from the reluctant pockets of unsaved people to support what is professedly of God!

To sum up: We have seen that an assembly of believers, according to the New Testament, gives room for the manifestation of all the gifts given by the Head of the Church for the edification of the assembly. In the fourth chapter of Ephesians, the Spirit of God, after describing the gifts given by Christ to His mystical body, reveals the purpose for which they were given (v. 12), and then describes the effect of these gifts in the assembly. We read: *"From Whom the whole body, fitly joined together and compacted by that which every joint supplieth, according to the effectual working in the measure of every part, maketh increase of the body unto the **edifying of itself in love**"* (Eph. 4:16).

Thus the evangelists in a local church should be busily engaged in preaching the gospel to the unsaved. The teachers should be faithfully seeking to instruct the believers. The pastors should be lovingly shepherding the flock among which the Holy Spirit has made them overseers (1 Pet. 5:1-4). The bishops or elders and deacons should be sincerely fulfilling their God-given functions. Is this possible in the assembly of which **you** form a part; or are you associated with a humanly conceived, humanly organized and humanly directed assembly, that allows no liberty for the exercise and development of the gifts given to the Church to function within the local assembly?

GOSPEL ACTIVITY BASED ON GOD'S WORD

EIGHTH: **Their gospel activity is governed by the principles laid down in God's Word.**

From the assemblies of those known as "brethren" thousands have gone forth to preach the gospel in the foreign mission fields, looking alone to the Lord for their support. As many more are busily engaged in the homelands opening up new places where little or no clear gospel is heard, and where these scriptural principles of gathering are not known or practised. Besides those who spend all their time in the Lord's work, there is a large army of business and professional men and tradesmen who devote their spare time to preaching the gospel, distributing tracts, visiting the sick and teaching the Word of God.

The only difference between these and the other workers is that they are part-time, and the others are whole-time labourers in the same harvest field. In every place where any of them are scheduled to preach the gospel, you may be absolutely certain of hearing nothing but the clear statement of man's need and God's remedy, and the proclamation of a full and free salvation, conditioned through faith in Christ's finished work, acceptance of Him as Saviour, and confession of Him as Lord of life (Rom. 10:9-10).

Go where you will in this world, and you will be certain of this: wherever these companies of Christians known as "brethren" are found, you will hear a scriptural presentation of the gospel that is honouring to God and glorifying to Christ. They are prepared, as individuals, to go **anywhere**, providing they can take the whole Bible with them, and are given liberty to declare the whole counsel of God. Wherever they go, they preach the word without fear, or favour, or charge. Eternity alone will reveal the countless thousands who have been led to own their need as sinners and trust the Saviour who has been presented to them through the gospel as preached by them.

Of course, each servant of the Lord is responsible, to his own Master alone, as to his **sphere** and **methods** of service (Rom. 14:4). While he should welcome advice from godly brethren, he should not allow himself to be dictated to regarding these things, for he is not *"the servant of man"* (Gal. 1:10). An ever increasing number of assembles, from which goes forth the Word with no uncertain sound, bear eloquent testimony to the fact that God's principles of gathering are as workable today as when they were laid down many years ago—providing God's people will bow to the authority of Scripture, and allow the Lord to have His rightful place as Head of the assembly, which is His body.

Being thus on scriptural ground, and acting upon scriptural principles of gathering, those that are added to an assembly thus gathered have freedom to develop their gift, and also to grow in grace and in the knowledge of their Lord and Saviour, Jesus Christ. One-man ministry tends to stifle this development of gifts, as also does narrow sectarianism and unscriptural principles.

A friend of mine once spoke to a very well known teacher among the denominations. During the conversation he asked him why it was that the average young Christian in an assembly of believers known as "brethren" could give a good scriptural definition and a clear exposition of the great doctrines of the Bible, while the average young Christian among the denominations could not. The worthy doctor of divinity, since gone home to be with Christ, though agreeing with the fact of the statement, could not furnish any explanation of its truth. My friend then pointed out that the explanation lay in the fact that those who met on scriptural principles were able to function according to scriptural principles, and a scriptural atmosphere was thus created that made possible the recognition, exercise and development of God-given ability.

GOSPEL ACTIVITY BASED ON GOD'S WORD

On another occasion, in Johannesburg, South Africa, an elderly clergyman, a true and godly Christian, came to the meeting for the breaking of bread and, of course, was received as a believer. After the bread had been broken and the cup passed, he arose and among other things, said: "Brethren, value the liberty you have in meeting thus, and let no one bring you into ecclesiastical bondage." Personally, the more I read and study the Bible, the longer I remain associated with those known as "brethren," the more I see of denominations and meet those who are linked to them, the clearer I see the scripturalness of the position of those who meet as believers only, and thank God that He ever, in His grace, led me to gather among them.

As companies of believers we freely admit to having failed in many respects, and bemoan the oft manifestations of the flesh among us, which has grieved the Holy Spirit and brought shame to the testimony of our Lord. We have to confess our lack of love oft times to those of our brethren with whom we have not seen eye to eye; but, in spite of all the failure, those known as "brethren" are seeking humbly and consistently to put into practice those principles of gathering found in the New Testament scriptures. Because of this fact, I do not want to be anywhere else but among those who seek to gather in the alone and sufficient name of the Lord Jesus Christ, and who accept the Word of God as the sole authority for faith and practice.

CONCLUSION: PRIVILEGES AND RESPONSIBILITIES OF ASSEMBLY FELLOWSHIP

The foregoing eight reasons for my being associated with those known as "brethren" really represent the **privileges** of being so gathered, but privilege always carries with it a corresponding **responsibility**. Since these principles of gathering are scriptural, it requires each Christian to act as before, the Lord in the light of them. I would suggest that each believer give his earnest and undivided attention to the four statements which follow.

First. Each genuine believer, who is sound in life and doctrine, and who realizes, from the Scriptures, the unscriptural character of denominationalism and all that it involves, will not rest until he or she is meeting with those who hold and practice these scriptural principles of gathering. Remember, it is not a case of "joining the brethren." If you are saved, the Spirit of God has already joined you to the body of Christ. It simply consists of intelligently and deliberately associating oneself with those who have **seen** and are **acting** upon the truth of the one body of which Christ is the Head, and every believer a member. The person who really apprehends this truth will never rest content until he has gladly gone forth from that which, in practice, denies Christ the place of pre-eminence in the assembly, and the Spirit of God the liberty to minister through whomsoever He will in the assembly. The scriptural assembly of believers, to whom you make known your decision, will gladly welcome you and exhort you to the right hand of fellowship after a godly sort.

Second. It will mean that he who has seen his privilege and has taken his place thus will surely desire to support the assembly by his presence at all its meetings whenever possible. He will earnestly cooperate with his fellow believers in the assembly and, by his wholehearted support financially, and his sacrificial efforts individually, will seek to encourage, strengthen and edify the company of believers with whom he meets.

There is a noticeable lack of this on the part of some who apparently imagine that their responsibility to an assembly ends with their being present at the meeting for the breaking of bread on the Lord's day. It needs to be emphasized that the prayer meeting, the Bible reading, and the gospel meeting, and the special meetings are just as much meetings of the assembly, as the feast of remembrance.

How can an assembly hope to develop spiritually if the prayer meeting is neglected? How can it be edified if a mere handful attend the Bible reading? What will the unsaved think, if only a few of the believers gather to support, by their presence and prayers, the one who is to deliver the gospel message? Only an excuse that can stand the light of the judgement seat of Christ should be made for not attending these meetings; yet the most trivial excuses are often put forth by those whose lack of heart, or ignorance of these principles, causes them to absent themselves from these meetings.

A Christian man whom I know, used to put it thus: "What kind of an assembly would this one be, if everybody in it was just like me?" Would there be a prayer meeting? A Bible reading? A gospel meeting? An assembly is formed by a **number** of believers, and the spiritual tone of the assembly is determined by the spirituality **of each individual** composing that assembly. When a person avoids the prayer meeting, it is a sign he needs that meeting more than anything else. Many a discouraged believer has been tempted to stay home on a prayer meeting night because he was tired in mind and body; but when he went, he discovered how true was the promise: *"They that wait upon the Lord shall exchange their strength"* (Isa. 40:31). Perhaps the very word of comfort or rebuke that we so much need is waiting for us at the Bible reading, but we must be there to get it, or it will do us no good.

If I would emphasize one thing above another to young believers in assemblies, it would be this: Be loyal to the assembly of which you form a part. Do not be a **liability**, be an **asset**. Do not go visiting around here and there on your own meeting night, or get so involved in other Christian work **outside** the assembly that you have no time to be present at its regular meetings and fulfill your obligations to your own home assembly. Concentration is a splendid thing. I have known an assembly to die because those composing it assumed no responsibility to it, and devoted their energies in this work and that effort, in many cases under denominational auspices, which were opposed to the very scriptural principles they professed to hold.

If the assembly with which you are connected is scriptural in its principles, **back it up** by all means in your power, and concentrate your energies on edifying, or building up that which is according to the pattern revealed in the New Testament. It is a case of either **concentration**, or **dissipation** of energy. Do not develop into a "sermon taster," or become a "floater," or a "thrill hunter," following this or that man around, to the neglecting of your own responsibilities in your home assembly. The story is told of a man who saw a boy about to drown a dog. On being asked why he was going to drown the dog, the boy replied: "Well, it's like this. The dog follows everybody, and a dog that follows everybody is good to nobody!" The moral is obvious.

Third. The Christian who seeks to gather according to these scriptural principles will need to have a big heart for all the children of God, by whatever name they may call themselves. He will have to continually challenge himself to distinguish between personalities and principles. He may not be able, in loyalty to the Word of God, to have fellowship with the system or sect with which this or that Christian is connected; but he ought to show that believer, as an individual, all the love and care that is due as one of "the brethren." It is sadly possible for an individual or an assembly who professes to have seen these scriptural principles, to become very sectarian in heart. Let us remember that all who "belong to Christ" are dear to His heart, and are in the Church which is His body. As such they should be the objects of our love. Our Lord's words should be deeply pondered in the heart: *"By this shall all men know that ye are My disciples, by your love one for another"* (John 13:35).

Any true Christian, who is morally clean as to his walk and sound in the fundamentals of God's Word should be **gladly welcomed** to the Lord's Supper, on no other condition than that he "belongs to Christ." To impose any other conditions of reception to an assembly **is to form a sect** with all its attendant evils. There is no such thing in Scripture as the sect of the "The Brethren"; but there is such a thing in Scripture as brethren being assembled together on the common ground of the head-ship of Christ and the unity of all believers as members of the body of Christ.

Any assembly that **knowingly** refuses a believer, who is sound in life and doctrine, a place at the Lord's Supper becomes, by that very act, **a sect**, however strenuously those composing it may deny the fact. Let us beware of sectarianism in any form! What mischief—and worse—has been wrought by a narrow, bigoted attitude adopted towards the Lord's people! If they belong to Christ, and are walking as becomes believers, count it the greatest privilege to welcome such, and so *"keep the unity of the Spirit in the bond of peace"* (Eph. 4:3). All snobbery is detest-able, but religious snobbery is the most nauseating of all. May the Lord give us to realize what a hateful thing it is to Him who *"loved the church and gave Himself for it"*! A well known teacher once wrote: "If you fail to provide an amount of fellowship for every known child of God, that moment you deserve to go out of existence" (J. N. D.).

Fourth. The believer who meets on scriptural principles should so study his Bible that he will be able to help other Christians who are not similarly placed as to their church asso-ciation. One has no need to apologize for this position among the so-called "brethren." Since it is of God, and according to

58

His Word, **let us boldly affirm it**, and seek to deliver our fellow believers from the evils of sectarianism, with its ordained clergy and all the confusion that goes with it. Plenty of good literature has been published on this subject by able teachers, so that there is no excuse for not knowing the certainty of the things we stand for. While careful to make no claims for perfection in our behaviour while so meeting, let us, however, boldly maintain the scripturalness of the principles that we seek to hold and practice.

A well-known teacher among the denominations once confided to me: "I'll come among you when you brethren cease your quarrels." At the time he said this, his own denomination was in the midst of a fearful row over the question as to who should govern its church policy, the modernists or the fundamentalists! Apparently this quarrel did not enter into his thoughts, or cause him to leave his denomination!

As "brethren," we have differences of opinion but, thank God, they are not over fundamental truths that question the inspiration of God's Word, or the Deity of Christ, etc. We do not have to dispute about the pastor's salary, being raised or lowered, or whether a modernist preacher shall be allowed to speak on our platform or not, or how we shall get rid of an unsaved "minister." All our differences can be solved by submitting to Scripture and manifesting that love, forbearance and humility the Word of God enjoins upon all the brethren. Let us then heed the injunction of Paul to Timothy: *"The things that thou hast heard of me amongst many witnesses, the same **commit thou to faithful men** who shall be able to **teach others also"** (2 Tim. 2:2).

May we so study and obey God's Word, that we shall each be found in the place where our Lord would have us to be, gathering in His name along with those whom it has pleased Him to call "His brethren"; owning to the authority of His Word; welcoming all true believers sound in doctrine and life; and allowing the Holy Spirit liberty to minister through whomsoever He will, to the glory of God and the edification of the assembly!

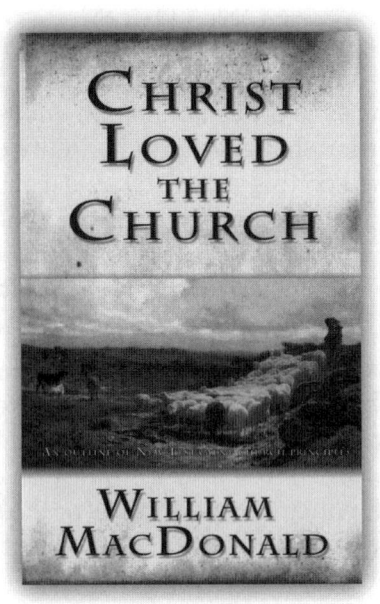

CHRIST LOVED THE CHURCH
by William MacDonald

What should the church be like? Is there an obvious, consistent picture of the church in the Bible? Was that kind of congregation intended as the pattern for generations of Christians following? Can it be lived two thousand years later? The author answers, "yes, yes, yes, yes." This is not a theoretical book. Bill MacDonald has witnessed others carrying out the New Testament pattern for church life in countries around the world. He has practiced and promoted these same principles, and happily, he knows how to communicate on paper.

Bill MacDonald shows how the Bible itself clears away the rubble of human tradition, and religious ritual. The Bible itself presents a clear mandate for assembly life where the true authority of the Head at God's right hand is known, loved and served. When you discover the Head of the Church in this way, you will also love His people. Do you love the body of Christ? You can. You should.

ISBN: 9781897117606 • B-17606 • 108 pages

THE CHURCH AT WORK
by Brian Gunning

The Christian life is do-able. God's design for the Church is not only a good theological idea—revealing the Lord to us—it is also a very practical idea—it works, following the biblical blueprint and working along with the Designer Himself.

Included in this very helpful, hand-on-book:

- God's Great Idea
- Practical Priesthood
- Giving & Receiving Correction
- The Joys of Hospitality
- 7 Mysteries of the Lord's Supper

- Unity-Watch It!
- Health Food for the Soul
- Our Place in History
- Roles of Men & Women
- Let Your Men Keep Silent

ISBN: 9781882701629 • B-CAW • 184 pages